W9-BRB-285

Funny, You Don't Look Like a Grandmother

Avon Books are available at special quantity discounts for bulk purchases for sales promotions, premiums, fund raising or educational use. Special books, or book excerpts, can also be created to fit specific needs.

For details write or telephone the office of the Director of Special Markets, Avon Books, Inc., Dept. FP, 1350 Avenue of the Americas, New York, New York 10019, 1-800-238-0658.

"Funny, you don't Look Like a Grandmother"

Lois Wyse

Illustrated by Lilla Rogers

AVON BOOKS • NEW YORK

Grateful acknowledgment is hereby given to *Good Housekeeping* magazine for permission to reprint the following pieces: "Grandma Mc," "Diary of a Mad Grandmother," "What Do You Give a Grandmother?" "Very Kathy," "Family Dinner," "Molly Is a Genius and Other Family Truths," "A Star for Marisa," "Is Your Grandmother Married?" "An Unmarried Grandmother," "What Price Grandma?"

AVON BOOKS, INC.
1350 Avenue of the Americas
New York, New York 10019

Text copyright © 1989 by Lois Wyse
Illustrations copyright © 1989 by Lilla Rogers
Cover illustrations and design © 1988 Lilla Rogers
Published by arrangement with Crown Publishers, Inc.
Library of Congress Catalog Card Number: 88-20387
ISBN: 0-380-70989-9
www.avonbooks.com

All rights reserved, which includes the right to reproduce this book or portions thereof in any form whatsoever except as provided by the U.S. Copyright Law. For information address Crown Publishers, Inc., 225 Park Avenue South, New York, New York 10003.

First Avon Books Trade Printing: May 1990

AVON TRADEMARK REG. U.S. PAT. OFF. AND IN OTHER COUNTRIES, MARCA REGISTRADA, HECHO EN U.S.A.

Printed in the U.S.A.

ARC 20 19 18 17 16 15

If you purchased this book without a cover, you should be aware that this book is stolen property. It was reported as "unsold and destroyed" to the publisher, and neither the author nor the publisher has received any payment for this "stripped book."

For
the family of grandchildren
Lee, our children, and I
will always love.

CONTENTS

INTRODUCTION

here are more grandmothers alive today than at any other time in the history of the world.

However, today's grandmothers don't look like grandmothers.

They look like women.

And that is what is so confusing.

My grandmothers were the real grandmothers.

They helped my grandfathers in their stores, had babies, made soup (my mother's mother) and icebox cookies (my father's mother).

My two grandmas wore dresses big enough and dark enough to cover their fleshy hills and valleys, those rippling results of their own cooking.

They did not know from gyms, exercise, or second marriage.

Also they did not know from gorgeous.

In the kitchen, who needed a bikini?

But in the last half of the twentieth century, grandmas have been on the move.

So long, unmade beds.

Good-bye, flower beds.

Today's grandma is out there selling real estate, flying planes, creating businesses, writing best-selling novels, acting, playing tennis, and zapping around Paris with or without a husband.

You can tell she is a grandmother, however, because in between all this action, she will call her daughter (to whom she gives advice which is always disregarded) and her daughter-in-

Grandma's toys

law (to whom she gives no advice because she knows it will be disregarded).

A mother becomes a true grandmother the day she stops noticing the terrible things her children do because she is so enchanted with the wonderful things her grandchildren do.

But under the size-six tennis dress, and inside the Saint Laurent sweater, between the sheets in the condo in Florida, and on the skis in Vail beats the heart of a grandmother.

How can you tell?

Just look...and listen....

On Becoming a Grandmother

(Notes from the front)

What Will We Name the Grandmother?

from the day they tell you the home pregnancy test was positive until the day they tell you the baby is here, you will be allowed to consider the single most complex naming problem you are permitted to solve: what will the new baby call you.

Never mind that the new baby will not call you anything for quite a while. Never mind that even when the baby does talk, the name will be garbled. Still you have to decide what Baby will call you.

It is wise to remember immediately that you will not be asked what to name the baby. Instead the children will ask what you will name yourself for Baby.

You will remind the children that you did not have to rename yourself when they were born. But your children are not listening.

My friend Marianne, my first grandmother contemporary, is called Nana. In our family that name was taken; my mother is Nana, and one Nana is the family limit.

So, faced with the choice of Grandmother or Grandma, I became Grandma. And because I am one of those grandmas whose last name isn't the same as the children's, life was made simple by naming me Grandma Lois. It does offer a kind of permanence that last names no longer do.

13

Firstborn Stephanie once shortened my name to Mama Lolo, which I like, but her mother (sensing a lack of respect, I guess) moved it back to Grandma Lois.

My grandson Max calls me Mama because he calls his mother Mimi—names he has established by taking the last syllable of Mommy and repeating it for his mom and the last syllable of Grandma and doubling that.

One woman who shuddered perceptibly at the very words *grandma* or *grandmother* has decided to be called Mom's-mom. Still another, a midwesterner, is known as Chicago Mommy. An auburn-haired granny is differentiated from the children's other grandmother by the title The Red Grandmother.

My friend Annelle was supposed to be called Grandmama by her English grandson, but his first words to her were "Amama" —now her family name.

My very favorite naming story is about Ed and Ethel, who were called the Jewish names "Zaide" and "Bubbie" by their grandson Josh.

When Josh went to nursery school, he talked continually about his zaide and bubbie. He told of adventures with them, and when show and tell day came, he announced that he would bring in his bubbie and zaide.

When he walked in with Ed and Ethel, his nursery school teacher said, "Who are these people?"

"Bubbie and Zaide," he said proudly.

"But . . . but," she stammered, "I thought they were gerbils."

FUNNY . . .

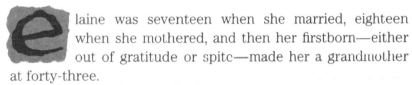laine was seventeen when she married, eighteen when she mothered, and then her firstborn—either out of gratitude or spite—made her a grandmother at forty-three.

Loudly she wailed, "But I'm too young to be a—a—," and then, realizing that the word she was about to say was not a word she cared to communicate to all the world, she whispered, "a grandmother."

The fact that most of her friends were grandmothers did not help. "You don't understand," she wailed to anyone who would listen, "I didn't plan on being a grandmother. You see, I planned to have these two adorable children, first a boy and then a girl. I would dress them in cute little matching clothes and take

them everywhere with me, and it would be picture-perfect. I wanted itsy-bitsy children. But look what my children did to me. First, they deceived me by becoming rotten teenagers, and then they got so old that they turned out to be older than I think I am, and now look what they've done! *Grandchildren.*"

Elaine does not hear when anyone says that clocks do not stop, children grow older not younger, and that while motherhood may indeed require a woman who says "yes," grandmotherhood does not.

"It's not so bad," her friends consoled her. "Look, you can always take your granddaughter shopping."

"I did, and that's the worst part," Elaine said glumly.

"Why?" asked her friend Dorothy.

"Because," Elaine explained, "when I take Missy shopping, people pinch her cheek and coo over her."

"Don't you like that?" Dorothy asked.

"Of course," Elaine said, "but the minute I try a little dress on Missy, the salesgirl rushes to say that Missy's mother will love it. So I always go on to explain that I'm the grandmother. After that they say, 'Funny, you don't look like a grandmother.'"

"So what's wrong with that?" Dorothy wondered.

"Don't you understand? They think it's funny I don't look like Missy's grandmother. But I think it's funny they never guess that I just might be Missy's mother. Once, just once, let some nearsighted clerk selling me a dress for Missy say, 'This will look lovely on your daughter.'"

Dorothy laughed. "Oh, Elaine, don't you understand why they know you're the grandmother? Who but a grandmother would walk right past all those little no-iron overalls and buy a handmade dress with six tiers of ruffles that takes a mother three hours to iron?"

GRANDMA ME

ho can ever imagine the sense of grandmotherhood?
Who can ever picture herself a rocking-chair granny?

Mommy, yes.

But grandmother? Certainly not I.

My children went to Lamaze and happy little parenting classes, but who tells us what it will be like?

Like all grandparents, I was given a warning of some months about the event, but who can be prepared?

The first person to clue me into the world of grandparenthood was my friend Isabelle. We were lunching, and somewhere between the salad and the coffee, I broke the news. Yes, I was very thrilled. Yes, I was ready. Yes, I understood what it would mean.

Isabelle listened and then sat back and smiled knowingly.

I was bewildered by her smugness.

"You only think you know," she said sagely. "Wait. Just wait. No matter what you expect, you won't be prepared."

She was right.

I wasn't prepared when the call came at 4 A.M. that the baby would be born within hours.

I rushed to the airport, caught a 7 A.M. plane, and ran for a cab to take me to the hospital. I did not telephone from the airport to learn what happened (I could not bear to hear about

this birth from an impersonal voice on the telephone).

I went immediately to the maternity-floor waiting room, where all our family was assembled, and I heard those wonderful words. "It's a healthy girl born ten minutes ago."

So.

Ten minutes old and already this little girl was arriving ahead of me.

Moments later, in her father's arms, the baby came to meet us.

To my shock and amazement I burst into tears. But not just ordinary, run-of-the-mill tears. This was old-fashioned, heart-rending sobbing. For in that moment I was touched by every life that had preceded this new one.

My father, dead before even my son was born, was there. So, too, were my grandparents, great-grandparents, uncles, aunts, cousins. In a great, convulsive tide I was swept back to my beginnings—child, young wife, mother.

I was filled with the enormity of that sense of belonging, all of us, each to the other. We are bound by our own inexorable, nonending saga. We are the human story. We are us. And now she is us. And only God knows what lies ahead of us—and all life.

No wonder I cried inconsolably.

No wonder my friend could not describe it.

INHERITANCE

China cupboards filled with cups of memories,
A piano's tune that sang its note before me,
Secret drawers that hold my parents' past,
All these are here for me to see
And so piece together what has gone before
To understand the people who once walked these halls.

For in the home my grandmother created,
I find the beginnings of the love I have inherited.

OH, GRANDMA,
WHAT LONG LUNCHES
YOU HAVE!

Barbara and Polly have a lot in common. They work at the same place, earn the same salary, and like the same movies. So how can you tell which one is the grandmother?

Easy.

The one who goes to garage sales on her lunch hour, calls home to see if the baby vomited, and rushes to take the egg salad sandwich to her child who forgot lunch—she's the mother.

The one in the darling little suit with the perky white flower in her lapel, the one who sits ordering her quiche and white wine while unfolding those endless pictures of adorable kids—she's the grandmother.

Nothing separates the generations like lunch.

Mothers are the ones who dine at the sink (they're not calories and they're not fattening so long as you don't sit down) gobbling leftovers and drinking diet soda.

Grandmothers are the ones who wait in line at the best restaurants for the best tables, and they care about fattening, too. So sometimes they'll have just a leaf and an olive for lunch. But on days when they do go for it, on days when they say, "Why not? Let's live a little," and have things like wild sauces and crème brulée—on those days they just breathe a little deeper and rush off to fancy gyms, where for the price of nursery school tuition, they roll their tummies back into shape.

Mothers, on the other hand, after splurging on double helpings of peanut butter, get back into shape by following exercise videos at home.

Grandmothers at lunch discuss the accomplishments of their children and what to buy the grandchildren.

If two mothers happen to lunch together, they rarely discuss anything beyond Heloise's suggestion for removing ketchup from the backseat of a Volvo.

A mother's idea of a relaxing lunch is going to a drive-in with her child's best friend so that for eight or nine minutes no one will even notice that she orders her double french fries with mustard.

So even though Barbara and Polly share their politics, books, and mascara, they know the one thing they will never share is lunch.

THE PLASTIC GRANDMA, OR SHOPALONG CASSIDY IS ON THE LOOSE

a grandmother, as her daughter and daughter-in-law know, is made of plastic credit cards.

There is not a grandmother worth her MBA (Major Buyers' Award) who confuses her presence with her presents.

So when grandmamas get together on the tennis court, at the office, or over a cup of coffee, these are some of the stories they tell, war stories from the front lines in every shopping mall in America, and from Madison Avenue to Rodeo Drive.

Sherry took her year-old son to get some shoes, and as she walked through the department store she saw a display of leather bomber jackets in Junior's size.

"These are the cutest things I've ever seen," Sherry said to the salesperson. "I'd love one for my son. How much are they?"

"One hundred and eighty dollars," was the reply.

"One hundred and eighty dollars," Sherry echoed as she reeled back in shock. "Who would ever pay that?"

"Grandmothers," said the salesperson.

It was Dawn's fourth birthday, and her grandmother was stumped. So she called Dawn's mother and asked the big question, "What shall we get for her?"

Dawn's mother confessed that they wanted to give her ballet lessons, and if Grandma wanted to pay for some of those . . .

"Perfect," said Grandma. "I'd love to do that, but I can't hand a four-year-old child a check. I want to give her a present. I think I'll get her a tutu."

Now it was Dawn's mommy's turn to say, "Perfect."

Grandma asked her friends and learned that the local toy store had a whole ballerina outfit—from tutu to crown. So, to double-check before shopping, she picked up the telephone and called the toy store.

"I want to buy a tutu," Grandma said. "What department is that?"

"Oh," said the operator, "you'll find the tutu in the twain department."

Jimmy came to New York to spend a day with his grand-mother. She took him to the park, the zoo, the planetarium, and three museums. By the fifth day she was running out of places to go.

"What are we doing today?" Jimmy asked.

Grandma thought for a moment. "I know," she said brightly, "let's go to a museum."

Jimmy's face fell. "We did that," he said.

"But this one," Grandma promised, "is different. This is the Toy Museum."

He jumped up and down. "The Toy Museum?"

"Yes, and before we go, I want to remind you about the two rules in all museums. You remember: no touching and no buy-ing. So you can see all the toys, but you can't touch, and you can't buy."

When Jimmy went home, he told his mother that he and

Grandma had had a really good time, but the best part was the Toy Museum.

When Mommy talked to Grandma, she said, "I don't remember the Toy Museum in New York. Jimmy loved it. Where is it?"

"Oh," Grandma explained, "that was F.A.O. Schwartz."

DIARY OF
A MAD GRANDMOTHER

hello," she said.

Immediately I knew there was something wrong.

She was boiling mad, and I could hear the steam escaping. Steam was escaping even in the word *hello*.

I knew I had to give her a safety valve.

But I didn't know I'd take the lid off the kettle just by asking, "What's wrong?"

"Wrong?" she snapped. "Don't ask me what's wrong. Ask me what's the good news and what's the bad news."

"Whatever you want. Okay. First give me the good news."

"The good news," she said grimly, "is that my daughter's bringing the baby and coming to visit.

"The bad news," she continued, "is that my daughter's bringing the baby and coming to visit. So not only do I have to go out and buy a crib, a car seat, outfit a nursery, and get baby food— all of which I am happy to do, very happy to do. But my daughter, my dear daughter, also expects me to babysit. Me!" she exploded. "Me with my calendar—imagine me becoming a babysitter in my twilight years."

"Twilight years?" I laughed. This is one of those friends who came on grandmotherhood at an age when some women are finding motherhood for the first time. "You have to be teasing," I assured her and me. "Come on. You're my tennis-playing pal."

"That's what I mean. Doesn't my daughter realize that I have a life of my own? Doesn't she realize that I work three days a week, play tennis once a week, belong to a reading group, and volunteer at the hospital? Didn't anyone tell her that while she took her time finding herself and going from school to school and job to job and finally settling down, getting married and having a child—doesn't she understand that all the time she was looking for herself out there, I was out there, too, and I was looking for me?

"Doesn't she know that I finally found me, and I am in some very interesting places?

"Doesn't she know there is life after grandmotherhood?"

I clucked sympathetically once or twice, and then I replaced the receiver, sat back, and thought about all of us who have watched our children struggle to become. And all the while we, too, have become.

I thought about all of us women and how we spend half our lives rebelling against our mothers and the next half rebelling against our daughters.

I wondered if we are always doomed to walk a path where only occasionally the destinations are the same, only occasionally the travelers in agreement on the road taken and the road not taken.

A few days later as I was reflecting still on my friend and her concern over her daughter's lack of understanding, the telephone rang. It was my friend once again.

This time the hello was on a low mellow note.

"Are we playing tennis after all?" I laughed.

"Tennis," she said in mock disgust. "Who would play tennis when there is the most adorable blond blue-eyed baby waiting to be held and played with and looking like—"

"But I thought you didn't want to babysit," I interrupted.

"Me? Not want to babysit? You must be kidding. This child is so adorable I beg my daughter to leave the house every morning so I can have her all to myself. She is the cutest, the most precious—"

"But your job, your reading group—"

"Oh, those things. They'll all be there next week, but this darling baby won't. One thing about me," she said in that righteous tone I have learned to expect in those who, after stumbling in the dark, find they own the light, "I know what's important."

THE
GRANNY WARS

hey are seated at a corner table in a little neighborhood restaurant, Rhoda and Doris and Marlene.

"Doris and I are taking you to lunch," Rhoda explains to Marlene, "because we think it's so wonderful that you're a granny now, too. And we want to tell you about some of the things that make it all work. So here we are with the best advice you'll ever get."

"We love taking new grandmas to lunch," Doris says, "because when our children got married, we knew we'd have to be good friends, and I really think that our friendship helped our

children get along. After all, Marlene, what's more important than family relationships?"

"So here we are, the mommy's mother and the daddy's mother, with just the teensiest hints," Rhoda promises. "Now to begin, it's very easy to keep peace in the family. Even though it's my daughter, I never feel free just 'dropping by.' So I'll tell you now, Marlene, never do that."

Doris, listening carefully, grimaces. Once—just once—she "dropped by," but only because she "just happened to be driving past the house." But when the door opened, and she was greeted with the Big Chill, she vowed never to do it again, and hasn't. Still she has never mentioned the event to a soul, not even to her husband. But now she squirms to know that her daughter-in-law rushes to tell her mommy everything. Oh God, and just when she thought that she and her daughter-in-law might have a real relationship after all.

Marlene pushes her coffee cup one inch to the left and says nothing.

Doris decides to break the uncomfortable silence. "About your house, Marlene, here's some advice. You just have to make up your mind that a baby can't deal with all that beautiful crystal you keep on your tables, and we all know that you can never reprimand the child or the mother becomes hysterical" —said with an indulgent smile toward Rhoda—"so when the baby comes to visit, let me tell you now that my best advice is to clear the tables and then just let the baby enjoy himself."

Rhoda bites her lip and does not speak. This, of course, is an oblique reference to the fact that Little Mutual at the age of three still can't be trusted in anybody's living room—an oblique reference to L.M., but a direct slap at Rhoda and the overly permissive way she raised her daughter, the reason that her

grandson moved without stopping from the Terrible Twos into the Threatening Threes.

"But at least he has a place to play at *my* house," Rhoda says at last.

Doris glares. Another reference, not veiled this time, to the fact that Doris lives in an apartment (Rhoda always manages to say the word apartment so that it sounds a little dirty) instead of a house like Rhoda's.

Marlene concentrates on pouring cream into her coffee and does not speak.

"Some grandmothers," Doris says with a tight smile, "think they can buy their grandchildren's affection. But what you learn very quickly, Marlene, is that the bigger the present, the more the child likes playing with the box and the ribbon and throwing out the toy. My advice is to give the baby a pan and a clothespin, and just watch him have fun."

Rhoda sniffs and does not speak. To herself she says, "I know what Doris means by *that*. That's her underhanded way of saying that she doesn't care that we buy those children everything they need—everything, absolutely everything—"

"Furthermore," Doris says, "money can't buy everything. For instance, it can't buy a child's love."

"I never tried to buy love," Rhoda says quickly. "But I learned in raising my own children that it isn't money that spoils children, it's permissiveness. What do you think, Marlene?"

Marlene is now searching the sugar bowl for artificial sweetener. She looks up and gives an artificially sweet smile to Rhoda.

"So. You agree," Rhoda says triumphantly.

"It's true we gave up a lot for our children," Doris says, "but that's how it was in those days. You have to remember that we wanted our son to have a good education. We knew he'd have

to earn a living someday and support a family." The last three words are said slowly and deliberately.

"My daughter," Rhoda says, "didn't need a man to support her. She had a job when she married your son."

"But what did she earn? Did she earn enough to buy those expensive shoes she wears or those vacations she always took?"

"If she hadn't taken that expensive vacation, she never would have married your son, and then—"

"And then," Marlene says quietly, "you two never would have had that wonderful grandson to love and cherish together."

"That's right," says Rhoda, "we do love Vincent, don't we, Doris?"

"He's a doll," says Doris, "even though the name Vincent was never my idea of a name for him."

WHAT DO YOU GIVE
A GRANDMOTHER?

There he was on television, just another one of your average Main Street kids (carefully culled from a bunch of ten-year-old millionaires who live in New York and California and make a bundle for themselves and their families by appearing on commercials).

This Typically American Kid with a Typically American Face wandering through a Typically American Store was saying with that Typically American Quizzical Television Introduction: What do you give a grandmother?

The kid, with the burdens of life known only to other kids in

television commercials, went on from there to explain that it was really tough for a boy to give a grandmother a gift, so he was sending his grandmother an American Express gift certificate.

Now, I have nothing against American Express.

I have an assortment of their cards in various colors that I use from time to time. I am proud to be a card-carrying grandmother, and I admit using that card to buy important and not-important grandchild gifts. But when the day comes that one of my grandchildren doesn't know what to give me—other than a gift certificate—I will turn in my American Express card and resort to something un American like cash.

Where are we if grandchildren are not raised to understand that there is a list as long as life and as deep as love to give to grandmothers?

What do you give a grandmother?

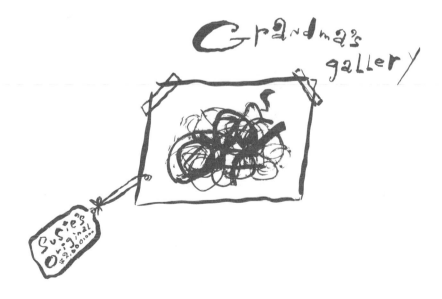

Well, American Express, here's what this grandmother loves to get:

1. A handmade picture by the artist (signed, of course)
2. A personally designed card with Grandma's name featured prominently (spelled or misspelled—who cares?)
3. The latest photograph of Darling Grandchild
4. A frame to hold the latter
5. A leaf, flower, acorn, or dandelion picked by Darling Grandchild
6. Cookies, cupcakes, or Anything Else made by D.G.
7. A poem or story signed by the author
8. An invitation to lunch (if D.G. lives nearby)
9. A telephone call—whether or not it's a gift occasion—because what Darling Grandchild has to learn is that there isn't a grandmother—with or without credit cards—who doesn't value a grandchild's two words over his two cents.

THE SECRET
NO GRANDMOTHER
EVER TELLS

 etty was grinning with that special female smile that indicated she was in possession of some extraordinary information.

"What do you know that I don't?" I asked quickly.

"I just found out what it's like to be a grandmother," she said on a note of triumph.

"You've known for years," I admonished. "You've been telling me about your two grandbabies—"

"Ah yes," she agreed, "but then we had this third."

"And?"

"And now I tell you I know what grandmothering is about."

"You didn't really know with the other two?"

"No, I didn't. One was adopted, and we kept looking at that child and saying how lucky we were to have a baby."

"And with the second?"

"With that one, a premature baby, we kept looking at that child and saying how lucky we were to have a living baby."

"And this one is different?"

"Very. This is just an ordinary child. Don't misunderstand. No baby is ordinary—except, well, with our family history, this is just an ordinary baby. So I don't stand at the crib and talk about how lucky we are to have her. I just stand there and wait for her to think how lucky she is to have all of us."

"She hasn't indicated that yet, has she?"

"No," Betty sighed. "She just lies there on the same side she was on the last time I saw her. Now that I think of it, I've only seen one side of this baby's face. She just sort of—thunk—lies there, and we walk around and—"

"And?"

"And try to get used to the idea of having just an ordinary baby."

"But this new experience has made a real grandmother out of you?"

"Absolutely. This time I'm not trembling with the newness of life or shaking over the fragility of life. This time I'm just standing at the crib like a regular grandmother waiting for a baby to become a kid. After you've already had a couple of grandchil-

dren, this just-standing-at-the-side-of-the-crib routine seems kind of boring. Promise you won't tell anyone, but frankly, this New Baby Boredom is the secret part of grandmothering that nobody ever tells you about."

SCHOOL FOR GRANDMOTHERS

hen the phone rang, I could hear her mother's voice coaching her in the background. "Ask Grandma to come to Grandparents' Visiting Day."

"No," Marisa said firmly.

"Shhhhh. She's on the phone now. Come ask her."

"No." Now it was a whisper.

Gently, ever so gently, the phone was put back on the hook, and I was left holding a dead line.

Moments like that make me very happy that I am not the mother of a first-grader.

A few seconds later the phone rang again. It was Heidi's sweetest voice. "Marisa would like you to come to her school for Grandparents' Visiting Day."

"Heidi," I said to the mother of the reluctant inviter, "I have already heard her enthusiasm for my being there. But that doesn't make any difference. I'm going."

And that's how I happened to be sitting on a chair that put my chin on my knees and my back out of whack, with my granddaughter at my side explaining the book she was going to take from the library, a book about a tiger that escaped from a

Rousseau painting and was trying to find its place in the real world.

Whatever became of the Three Bears and full-size chairs? I wondered.

I found neither in our next class, reading. But there I did find another grandmother and two grandfathers. Each girl in the all-girl school had to introduce her grandparent, and at Marisa's turn I understood my granddaughter's ambivalence about my attendance at her school.

She was six years old and already anticipating the worst of both worlds. If her grandmother came, she'd have to be introduced and judged by Marisa's peers; and if she didn't come, Marisa would be forced to admit that she didn't own a grandparent who cared enough to come to see her in class.

The subject of today's reading story was crabs. We read about crabs being cracked and crushed, and pretty soon even the slowest grandparent among us (me) understood that today's lesson was about the "cr" sound. It's called a blend, in case anyone around five or six should ask you.

Writing class was where the girls really starred. Each one had written a paper about her grandparents.

What would Marisa write? I wondered.

Marisa, this tender and smart child, this wonder woman of little girls, what would she say about her grandparents?

The first student stood in front of the class to read her treatise. "I love my grandma. She gets toys for me. I say thank you."

The next child sounded like my favorite grandmother joke. "I like my grandmother because I ask my mother for a doll. My mother says no. I ask my grandmother. My grandmother says yes."

The next child read about receiving a pink bicycle from her grandmother.

I listened to these literary gems with lofty indifference. Marisa's piece will be so different, I assured myself. Marisa, our little golden child, will have written something provocative, something of depth. Would a child who reads of Rousseau be so callous as to think of grandparents only as producers of clothes and toys?

The answer is yes.

Marisa's essay in full was, "It's nice to have grandparents because they give me toys. and they give me beautiful drsses" (sic).

When I left school I walked up the avenue.

So.

This puts it all in perspective.

Marisa does not remember the family dinners, the picnics, the lunches, and trips. She does not remember the walks in the woods and the reading of stories and playing of games.

What's a modern grandparent to do?

I sighed deeply.

And then I saw it. The most perfect pink dress for a six-year-old going on seven. I walked into the store.

"That dress looks just like my granddaughter," I said loudly so everyone would know how adorable Marisa is.

The saleswoman nodded indulgently.

After all, it was Grandparents' Visiting Day at the school around the block. And when Marisa drew the picture that accompanied her deathless prose, she showed a closet half filled with pretty little pink dresses and the other half filled with empty hangers.

LISTEN TO
YOUR GRANDMOTHER

If all of life's lessons were in books, obviously there would be no need for grandmothers. But grandmothers are to life what the Ph.D. is to education.

There is nothing you can feel, taste, expect, predict, or want that the grandmothers in your family do not know about in detail.

All grandmothers assure you that they know how you feel before you do.

If it (good or bad) didn't happen to them, then it happened to their mothers or grandmothers, and they can tell the stories to back up their wisdom.

It always amazes children that grandmothers know things before they happen. For instance, a grandmother in Duluth told her grandson he would catch cold if he did not wear his sweater —and, of course, he didn't believe his grandmother, so he went out without his sweater on a sunny February afternoon, and the very next day was sniffling and sneezing.

The world is full of such stories.

Over the past years I have culled much grandmother wisdom (a great deal of it from overhearing the conversations of grandmothers addressing their sweet little grandchildren) and the best of the advice is reprinted here.

"Come to the phone when Grandma calls"
(Advice of Olivia P., Fort Wayne, Indiana)

"It's not nice to keep a grandmother waiting. Now I'm not telling you that anything terrible will happen to you if you keep me waiting, but once I heard about a little boy who made his grandmother wait and wait, and sometimes he said he was too busy playing to come to the phone. And you know what happened? You'll never guess!

"That year Santa Claus forgot where that little boy lived."

"Write to your grandma from camp"
(An illegally taped conversation from the phone lines
of Sylvia B., Boise, Idaho)

"I notice that your mother and father gave you stamped, addressed envelopes now that you're going to camp. One of those envelopes has my name on it, Wendy dear. Me. Grandma. And I hope you will write to me. Oh, of course I'll write to you, too. And I'll even send—well, I won't tell you what I'll send.

"Just let me tell you what happened to my cousin's granddaughter when she didn't write to her grandmother from camp. Well, my cousin didn't know her granddaughter's address at camp because she never heard from her, so she couldn't send her the boxes and boxes of cookies she had baked for her.

"All of the other girls in the cabin got cookies from their grandmothers, and they traded, but this little girl didn't have anything to trade, so nobody gave her cookies. Pretty soon she stopped eating. And to this day—she is now thirty-seven years old—would you believe that that granddaughter can't look at a cookie without crying and thinking how terrible she was to her grandmother.

"So please, dear, just a little line to let me know how you are."

"If you really want to know what life's about, ask Grandma" (An actual conversation between Timothy D. and his grandmother Marybeth M., which took place while making fudge in the kitchen at Grandma's house in Mansfield, Ohio)

"Well, Timothy, I hear that your teacher asked you to write an essay about your family. What's that? Did I go to school with anyone famous like Abraham Lincoln or Dolly Parton? No, I'm afraid not. We didn't even have a future councilman in that class.

"No, I didn't enlist in the Army. No, no, I didn't learn to fly when I was seventeen. Matter of fact, I still get butterflies when I have to go anywhere.

"Sorry, but I never did march in a parade for women's rights. And no, I didn't ever go to jail for my beliefs. No, no, I'm not the grandmother who climbed Mount Everest, and I certainly am not the grandmother who swam the Channel, won a dance contest, or served as a missionary in Africa.

"I'm afraid that I'm not going to be much of a story for you, Tim, because what I am is a pretty dull, boring grandmother . . . although it's never seemed quite that way to me. You see, I married Grandpop right after we both got out of school. And we did a thing that was kind of remarkable for our time—we stayed married. Even more unusual is the fact that we stayed in love. It never bothered me that my driver's license said 'Housewife,' because it seemed important to me to be able to watch a house full of children and be a wife to the man I loved.

"Back in those days some of the other mothers worked, but I was one of the ones who was waiting at home for the children after school. One little girl in your daddy's class used to call me

'Mrs. Milk and Crackers,' her way of saying Mrs. McCracken, I guess. But I was the mommy who was there with the milk and crackers.

"I didn't much like what I saw during those years my children were growing up, but I held my tongue. And now I've lived long enough to hear people—some even younger than I—say that there was too much foolishness and not enough old-fashioned discipline back in those years. Between you and me, Timmy, there's a lot going on these days that I don't much like either. But there are some things I do like.

"I do like the fact that your parents know that my home is always open to you children, and I do like the fact that you come back here for Christmas wherever you are.

"I like being a grandma, and I like being called that. None of those fake 'nonny, noony, baba' names for me. I like cooking in my very own kitchen and making popcorn and candy apples and lemon pie and knowing that you'll come over to eat it all. I like knitting scarves and socks and sweaters for my grandchildren, and I like it when you come to visit—and I love the peace and quiet when you leave.

"Truthfully, Timothy, and you can put this part in your essay. ... You can tell your teacher your granny said, 'I am comfortable with myself, and my only question at this time of life is, 'How many of those dieting-to-live grandmas, how many of those multi-married Ms.'s, how many of those grannies with wrinkles surgically removed wouldn't in their heart of hearts want to be able to relax, act their age, and be an old-fashioned rocking-chair grandma like me?'"

AGE-OLD
CONVERSATIONS

"Grandma, are you old?"
"Compared to what?"

I am continually amazed at how old young has become.

Didn't we, like our grandchildren, begin with a childhood we thought would never end? Now, all of a sudden, I'm older than my parents were when I thought *they* were old.

When I go to visit my mother, her friends turn and say, "Lois, you look like a kid," but I am forced to admit that only to my mother's friends do I look like a kid. To a kid, I don't look like a kid.

Age becomes reality when you hear someone refer to "that attractive young woman standing next to the woman in the green dress," and you find that you're the one in the green dress.

It doesn't make me feel old to carry pictures of my grandchildren, but it does make me feel old when I can't see the pictures without my glasses.

Grandchildren are the dots that connect the lines from generation to generation.

IS IT MY BIRTHDAY AGAIN?

I count my birthdays
With the detached digital determination
Of a computer.

The difference is
This computer has
No subtract capability.

And my add button
Has been replaced
By multiply.

WHO BUT A FRIEND?

they weren't going-to-high-school friends.
They weren't even early-days-of-marriage friends.
They didn't know each other when their children
were born.

But the four were all in place by the time their children's
children came into the world.

And that was the reason the three women—out of the goodness of their hearts and the charity of their spirits, of course—
called their faithful fourth, Babette, and invited her to lunch.

"Isn't that nice of them to take me out?" Babette asked her
husband rhetorically, which, as most wives know, is the most
satisfactory way to ask a husband a question.

Herbert agreed it was nice. At least she thinks he agreed.

And so on a lovely spring day with the promise that only a May day brings, Babs trotted off to luncheon with three friends.

Over the mushroom omelet and glass of wine, Babette confessed that she wasn't sure why they were taking her to lunch, but she thought it was a wonderful thing to do. So—so charming and friendly. A warm gesture in a cold, indifferent world.

The three looked at each other, that semi-guilty look that women exchange when their suspect motives are suddenly clothed in goodness.

Marcia thought it was time to speak out. "Babette," she said in her most careful tone, "don't you really know why we're here?"

Babs shook her head. "I know it's not my birthday, but I just thought—"

"Never mind what you thought," Linda interrupted. "I can't sit here and pretend any longer. Babette, we want to talk about —well, about you."

"How flattering," Babs said, her eyes downcast. She felt a small blush of pride. These three women, all so busy, all so attractive, taking such a special interest in her. It was a bit heady.

Patty shook her head. "You don't understand, do you, Babs? We're here because we want to help you."

"Do I need help?" Babs asked querulously.

"Yes," the three answered in unison.

"Why?" Babs wondered aloud. "What have I done wrong? Was it the fish mousse I served at our party last Saturday night? Was our Christmas letter too boring? Was it—"

"Stop," Linda commanded. "Now listen to us. Marcia, you tell her."

The hapless Marcia looked stricken, but it was a job someone

had to do. She might as well be the one. She started, "You're a fine hostess, a lovely wife, a loving wife. But frankly, Babette, you're driving us all crazy as a grandmother."

"I am?" she asked. "But how?"

"Babette, you have just become a grandmother, and you have just stopped being a woman. You're not a friend. You're not— well, let's put it all in plain English. You're no fun anymore. All you ever want to talk about is a six-month-old baby boy. We know he'll be an outstanding man. We know he'll be a credit to his family. But for heaven's sake, Babette, don't make us go through every diaper on his way to graduation from nursery school."

Babette looked in surprise at her three friends. "But I thought you all cared."

"We do," Linda assured her. "We do care, and if there is a piece of news of headline importance, we hope you'll share it with us. But meanwhile, please stop with the pictures and the feedings and the adorableness."

"I brought a lot of new pictures with me," Babette said hopefully. Then she looked at the three expressions of dismay around her. "But I promise not to show them to you. Not today anyway," she said weakly, closing the handbag on her lap. The faces did not change expression. "I won't show them at all," she said sadly.

"Good idea," Marcia said heartily. "In fact, it's a swell idea never to bring pictures with you when you go to a dinner party either."

Patty smiled. "Remember, Babette, when you came to our house for dinner, and I seated you next to Joe's roommate from Yale, the one who was the Rhodes scholar and was considering running for the Senate?"

Babette nodded.

"We thought that was the perfect combination. You're so worldly, and Joe was positive his old roomie would appreciate your company. But at the end of the evening, all he could say was, 'For God's sake, Joe, don't you know anybody more interesting than a new grandmother?'"

"I guess this means you like me or you wouldn't bother saying all this," Babette ventured.

"Absolutely," said Marcia.

"Definitely," said Linda.

"Without question," said Patty.

"You know what I'm going to do," Babette said. "I'm going to be very good with all of you. I'll never talk about my grandson again, but meanwhile I think I'm going to start the first chapter of Grandmothers Anonymous. It will be a kind of Alcoholics Anonymous for grandmoms like me who just can't help talking about those great kids."

"I think that's a wonderful idea," said Patty.

"And when you have your first grandchild," Babette said sweetly, "I am going to give each one of you an honorary membership."

THROUGH THE TUNNEL

there was a time when children went across the river and through the woods to Grandmother's house. But nowadays for grandchildren to visit us urban grandmas, it is through the tunnel and across the town (and always at the height of the rush hour).

And we come through that tunnel, my first grandchild Stephanie and I, full of anticipation for what our relationship will be.

She sees me, I suppose, in her preschool mind, as a source of pleasure.

And that is how I, in my postparental mind, see her.

Where we differ, of course, is on our definition of pleasure.

Stephanie's view of pleasure is from the floor up—the floor where she crayons, rolls over, plays, and runs wild.

My view is at least five feet above hers. And my definition of pleasure is one where I read, teach, expand her view, and run easy.

Is it any wonder we have trouble deciding how to spend our allotted time together?

Don't her parents know that is why I cannot say no to her? We start at such a great distance that I cannot add more distance by refusing her.

Our lives, our last-half-of-the-twentieth-century lives, are so complicated by train schedules and tunnel traffic and discipline that the times for knowing one another are compressed—something like those squeegee hard rubber toys that expand to full size in the bathtub—and our tub times are rare.

Still, there are times.

Like the time that Stephanie came with her daddy for an overnight at Grandma's.

We did the dumb things—ate pizza, baked brownies—and smart things—played with the computer, read—and then her father and I left her, ponytailed and pajama'd, ready for bed.

When we returned two hours later, the sitter said she was asleep. But in minutes there was a cry from the bedroom.

I went in, and there was Stephanie sitting up in bed, whimpering, "Cuddle me, Grandma."

My heart did a slow turn, and all the rest of me felt like vanilla ice cream that had just had hot fudge poured over it.

I picked her up at the moment her father walked in the room.

"Put her down," he said with parental concern. "You cannot give in to her."

"Yes, I can," I said quickly.

What my son doesn't realize is that the biggest give I can give Stephanie is the give-in. Bigger than toys and games and clothes. I cannot be her prime instructor in life. I cannot guide her, nor do I wish to.

All I can do is give in to her.

All any grandmother can do is give a grandchild what he or she wants when it is wanted.

Our children will have to learn something new—they will have to learn that the difference between parents and grandparents is that all of us grandparents can afford to break the rules because we don't make them.

Our children will have to come through the tunnel with their children and find that Grandma—for the first time—is on the other side for them, too.

FULFILLMENT: GRANNY'S GOAL

I f you were to ask either of my grandmothers if she were fulfilled, she would have shrugged her shoulders and told you that, of course, she was fulfilled. The children's stomachs were full, and the shelves were filled with the foods she canned.

Canning season came sometime between the fall of the first leaf and the first snow, and it was marked by the smell of fruits cooking, pickle brine, and the scalding of hundreds of mason jars.

We who are the granddaughters of that generation taught ourselves to believe that kitchen is a confining word. To our contemporaries the words "Occupation: Housewife" are verboten, and we are not permitted to be full or filled by the sounds and smells of the household. This is a generation that came of age during the women's movement and has had to cope with the greatest sociological changes since man began recording history.

We are the generation that carved a new definition of woman, a definition that gave us some excellent middle-management jobs and a strong taste of prejudice, discrimination, and anger. Executives found that we were very good in our jobs, and what made us even better was the fact that we were all willing to do more for less. It was those very virtues that made us the enemy of the working man.

We helped this new low-cost employment force (women began to look like the Far East of American help) gain credibility because through our magazines and speeches and leaders, we condoned a society that frowned on women who didn't work and assumed that any dummy (like our mothers) could raise a terrific kid. We looked for equality, and what we got was a new definition of equality: It said that woman was equal to doing man's work—and her own—and at the same time.

We created a beautiful myth about the woman who could have it all. She could be thin and rich and powerful.

We encouraged our daughters to enroll in women's study courses, and we talked about their futures and the way they would run their homes in the future.

And then, lo and behold! our daughters got married, and they wondered what we were talking about. They were so tired they couldn't even call us to complain. They were so busy running from the office to the house that they were each willing—personally—to march across Helen Gurley Brown's desk and tell her that she was full of beans. The only problem was they were too tired to march.

During those years (until last week, in fact) I was fond of saying that all women who were now thirty-five years old would want to switch 180 degrees in ten years. That is, I reported to anyone who would listen, all women who are thirty-five and in the work force on an upwardly mobile path would like to be at home with children in ten years, and all women now at home with children would, in ten years, like to be on an upwardly mobile career path.

I made the mistake of saying that in front of my daughter-in-law. "You're wrong," she said quickly. All children, I have learned, are quick to say, "You're wrong," slower to say, "You're right."

She went on to explain. "My friends—except for me—don't expect to go back to work. They like staying at home. They like playing with their children, and some of them even like cooking and entertaining. They never want to go to work again."

My daughter agreed. "The women in the park where I take my children don't want to go back to work. You know," she confided, "it's not that great working."

I've been thinking about this ever since our conversation the other night. I thought about it while I canceled a dinner to go out of town on business. I thought about it while I made early-morning coffee before rushing off to a breakfast meeting.

And, you know, just today I saw mason jars in the hardware store. I wonder....

YUP, YUP . . . AND
BABY MAKES THREE

From the outside you'd say they were just another terrific Yuppie couple. They met at college, considered life together, and finally went off to marry and raise a family in a sweet little New England town. It's all a kind of picture-book life in a picture-book America, him and her and a houseful of children.

But instead of one or two little darlings, they had no babies because long ago, in order to have a child, her mother had taken a then-miracle drug called DES. And the daughters of those mothers who took stilbestrol now face insurmountable fertility problems of their own.

The couple went from clinic to clinic, consulted doctors everywhere, and finally determined that their best solution was to adopt.

"It's easy to say," the prospective mother confessed as she faced still another heartbreak, "but there just aren't any cute little babies out there for cute little couples like us."

And then one day she called her mother. "We got a baby," she said proudly.

Her mother was thrilled.

"And he's Korean," she added.

Her mother was still thrilled, but her mother was not prepared for some of the comments of her friends.

"Really," they said in barely audible tones, "you can tell us. Don't you feel—well, kind of strange about it?"

"No," answered the new grandmother as she rushed to find if layettes still required the same kind of sleep sacs her children had needed.

"But the baby," another friend said confidentially, "what about the baby? He's not going to look like anyone else."

"I know," the new grandmother said, "and isn't that wonderful? It's enough that Sue and Jerry look alike. Now when you see the family picture, there will be little Christopher—this darling little Asian face. Come on, isn't that what America is all about?"

Little Christopher is two years old now, and—wonder of wonders—he is an older brother. In one of those sometime miracles, Sue became pregnant after Christopher came to them.

When Grandma called all her friends to announce the birth of the second child, she exclaimed with delight, "We have a new baby." Then she paused and added softly, "Guess what? He doesn't look like anybody else in the family either."

GRANDMOTHERS' RIGHTS

Grandmotherhood does not give us
The right to speak
Without thinking,
But only the right
To think
Without speaking.

On Becoming a Mother's Mother

Mother

(notes from the rear)

WHAT'S IN A NAME?

f I tell you that her name is Gloria, I do not have to add "And she's over fifty."

You show me a woman named Gloria who doesn't remember Shirley Temple and *Fantasia* from the first time around, and I'll show you a woman who lies about her age.

Gloria and her four best friends—Phyllis, Marilyn, Judy, and Shirley—were all born during the Depression to mothers with names like Rose, Elizabeth, Mary, Sara, and Tillie.

When Gloria and her best friends got married and had daughters of their own, they gave them names like Kathy, Pam, Heidi, Stacy, Sidney.

And now that Kathy, Pam, Heidi, et al., are old enough to have their own babies, what are they naming their daughters?

Rose. Elizabeth. Mary. Sara. And Tillie.

There must be a moral here.

Maybe names are like furniture.

First they're new and wonderful.

Then they're second-hand and second-best.

And then they are recycled to come back as genuine antiques, quaint and charming.

Stay tuned.

Obviously Rose, Elizabeth, Mary, and their friends are going to have a lot of little girls named Gloria.

On the other hand, not since Cher named her daughter Chastity and her son Elijah Blue has there been such a spate of non-names for children.

Non-names have no relationship to geographic genealogy. A grandmother has a New York grandson named Blaze and a California grandson called Shane. In Texas a granny calls, "King," and a boy, not a dog, comes running. In Chicago there is at least one grandmother whose grandson Duke was named for the family's favorite hound.

Calling children the names usually reserved for horses and dogs is mitigated only by the knowledge that animal owners are now calling their pets Lucy, Tom, George, and Sam.

"Duke"

The Next generation

Among the best-named animals in recent years is the cat whose owner named him Eliot—and plans to name the next one T.S.—so the owner can be assured a couple of long-running cats.

How do baby namings like this begin?

Well, it may well have begun with Tab Hunter and poked along for a couple of generations until it moved to the status of a trend.

Here, Spot.

No, not you; back to your cage, Herb.

A BOY FOR YOU
AND A GIRL FOR ME

Joyce always thought she was a good mother. Her children had vitamins and check-ups, camp and cars. She and Harry sent them to adequate schools (the only ones that would admit them), and when both married, she and Harry gave them each a substantial check, in keeping, of course, with the family's finances of the moment.

But do these children, these new suburbanites and recent parents both, think she is a good mother?

"It shocks me," Joyce confessed over tea, "but my children think I raised them all wrong. Listen to this....

"Just the other day I stopped by to see my daughter and brought her daughter a Barbie doll. I thought my daughter was going to turn turquoise when my granddaughter hugged and kissed the doll. My daughter snatched it away from her. 'Why?' I asked. 'Why?' my daughter fumed. 'I'll tell you why.'

"And then my daughter proceeded to do seven minutes on the evils of Barbie dolls, the rise of sexism, and my inability to recognize her three-year-old Debbie as a person, not a girl. Following that my daughter did six more minutes on how I ruined her life by telling her very early in her life that she was a girl. How would she have found out if I hadn't told her first?

"Well, after that whole scene with my daughter I figured I'd know just how to shop for my son's boy. The little boy is a person, right? We all know that, don't we? Two years old, and he is a person. My children did not give birth to children. No, my children gave birth to persons. I don't have a grandson and a granddaughter. I have two grandpersons. All right. So I went to buy the boy grandperson a toy. Nothing that would break the bank, you understand. I went to buy him a little toy just to let him know that Goo-goo—that's what he calls me—well, I wanted him to know that Goo-goo loves him. Keeping in mind that my daughter was hysterical because I gave her daughter a doll meaning she was a girl, I figured I will give my boy grandperson a gift meaning he is the new non-stereotyped person. Since girls can no longer play with dolls, he will be a boy who will play with dolls. Right? Wrong. I went to my son's house, handed Baby Grandperson a Minnie Mouse doll, and his father went berserk. 'Couldn't you at least buy him a Mickey Mouse doll? Don't you know that role models and role playing begin at an early age? Do you think I want my boy thinking he's a girl? Once when I was four years old, you let me play with your jewelry, and it took me five years of analysis to understand that all of my problems began at that moment. You never gave me a true sexual identity, and now you're doing the same thing with my child.' "

"What did you say?" I asked.

"Nothing," Joyce said glumly. "I just looked at him. Obviously parenthood has corroded the minds of my children."

Then Joyce's face brightened. "You know what? Someday when their children are grown, the girl grandperson will have a baby, and she will say to her mother as she prohibits her from seeing her new child, 'You can't see my baby because I know you don't truly like children. I learned that the time you wouldn't let my grandmother give me a Barbie doll.'"

"And the boy grandperson?" I asked.

"The boy grandperson will brandish his revolver as he says to his father, 'But you told Goo-goo no dolls, and that's how I got this gun.'"

VERY KATHY

I had a problem not long ago.

Not a life and death problem, but a problem none-theless. And I needed someone who could act as an advisor. I thought of friends I might call, but none of them would really have understood. And my problem wasn't the kind you'd take to a husband. It was really a woman's dilemma, born in the workplace and not at home.

Just when I wondered who could share this concern, my daughter Kathy called. "Just checking in," she said with that here-I-am-because-I-think-you-expect-me sound in her voice.

"I'm so glad," I said. "I need your advice."

"You need *my* advice?" she asked, surprised.

To tell the truth, I was as surprised as she. But I did need her counsel. Even more, I needed her understanding. And so she

listened. She listened very carefully and then proceeded to tell me what she thought. She didn't try to spare my feelings, nor did she try to hurt them. She truly tried to help. And because she tried to help, she did.

A few days later I was asked to speak at an advertising club in a town not far from where my daughter lives. I agreed to be the speaker if Kathy (also an advertising writer) might introduce me. Everyone thought it would be a lovely gesture.

We spent the day together, my child and I, and when the time came for her to introduce me, she looked at me—and I looked at her—and a flood of tender memories returned. This lovely, poised woman—was she really the little girl we reared?

I remember standing at the living-room window the year she was sixteen. It was 2 A.M., and she was out with the boy she was dating that year.

I thought I trusted her. I thought I trusted him.

Still, who knows what can happen when teens are driving?

She was due home at midnight, and she hadn't called. I was scared. I knew I shouldn't do what was on my mind—but I did it anyway. I called the police. And just as I was asking if there had been an accident reported, I heard the familiar crunch of car wheels in the driveway. I can't recall the reason she was late. All I can remember over the years is the sheer relief, the unbridled joy I felt when I knew Kathy was there, safe and sound.

I remember another earlier time, when she was six and accidentally pushed her hand through the storm door, and I rushed her to the hospital emergency room. ("One more inch to the side, and that child might not be here," the doctor said.)

But she was here.

We had fooled the fates.

We had survived.

Back and forth the memories went.

I remembered her wedding, so carefully planned, and I thought of the words she said the next day: "Mom, the wedding was perfect. And you were great—really nervous, just the way the bride's mother should be."

Funny, isn't it?

No matter how old our daughters are, we still ache and dream for them.

And we are still nervous.

Wasn't I nervous at that very moment?

For here in front of a large audience was my daughter ready to introduce me.

Later she gave me a copy of her remarks. It was a good thing she did because I never could have remembered them through the mist of the moment. She was sweet and tender and funny. But, most of all, she was very . . . well, very Kathy.

How do you thank a daughter for suddenly making you realize how much you value what you have together?

How do you let a daughter know that despite the irritation, the frustration, the anger and confusion of earlier years, you are aware of how rich she has made your life?

I was not sure I would know what to say to her, but when the day was over, I told Kathy that all I could wish her was the best thing a mother can wish—that someday a daughter will make her feel as fulfilled as she has made me feel.

On the day that Kathy's daughter Molly was born, I thought back to that special day with Kathy, and I wondered if Molly would turn out to be as good at introductions as her mother.

FAMILY DINNER

No matter the holiday, when we gather around the table we give new meaning to the word "family" because we are the latest word in relatives, an amalgam of his-and-her children, somebody's niece, an occasional nephew, a wandering friend, and at least two leftover uncles and aunts. ("Are they yours, his, or hers?")

Our family dinners are made of a patchwork guest list, and each time that we count heads, we know we are looking at a very different gathering from the tight nuclear family of years ago.

For we, my husband and I, are the progenitors of the next society. We are the creators and assemblers of The New Family.

The New Family is a collection of semi-related folk who are partly nonmarried, partly old-married, and partly remarriaged. And we have taken it upon ourselves to make the parts whole for the holidays.

We do not do this alone.

We are assisted by our children, who love all our family customs. At Thanksgiving, for instance, each one of us stands and tells those things for which he or she is thankful. It's teary and tender and quite wonderful. And each year when it is over, our children come to us and say, "Let's keep Thanksgiving small next year."

And then one or the other of them goes ahead and has another baby.

Our children who want to keep things small have given us

seven grandchildren in less than seven years.

But this is how the new math works in the new family.

When you have his children and her children bringing in their grandchildren, the babies never stop.

Everybody grows up being everybody's cousin.

And each grandchild is aware of a lot of love.

A generation ago there were children who never saw their grandparents, but now we have children who are rolling in grandparents.

Our Marisa and Elizabeth have three grandmothers.

Noah has had a loving relationship with his five grandfathers and six grandmothers (but not all at once, marriage and divorce being what it is).

Stephanie, Alex, Max, and Molly also have three grandfathers —but only one of them is the same as Marisa and Elizabeth's.

If you think you're confused, just stop by for a holiday dinner. No matter who you are, our grandchildren will just assume you're somebody's grandma.

Around our house everybody is.

GRANDMOTHER
KNOWS BEST

She's one of those long-stemmed Texas roses who became famous on two coasts, and while her days (and nights) as a beauty are not ended, she is now best-known for her absolute total dottiness over her firstborn grandson.

If you talk to her for five minutes, you will know all there is to know about grandson Maximilian (now, there's a name to hand down). But adore as she does this small boy, she aches for a granddaughter, too.

Why?

"Because," she explains, "the best advice I ever had on raising a daughter came from my grandmother, and I can't wait to give that advice to my daughter for her daughter.

"My grandmother understood that it was a mother's responsibility to make sure there would be a next generation. Therefore, a mother had to be certain her daughter was marriageable. My grandmother was totally committed to that belief.

"Now that we tried a generation of pooh-poohing marriage and found it didn't do any of us any good, it looks as if we're going to go right back to marriage, and I want to tell my daughter what to do for her daughter."

Ever the opportunist, I allowed that since my friend doesn't yet have a granddaughter and I have a slew of them, wouldn't it make sense to pass her grandmother's wisdom along to me so I might tell my daughter?

So here it is: How to Marry, Texas Style.

Rule #1: Maintain your body.

"My grandmother," explained my friend, "knew that no matter how fashion hid the body, man would find it. And if he didn't find it to his liking, woe to woman."

Rule #2: When your daughter is eighteen or twenty-two, make sure she's surrounded by the proper young men.

"Grandmother was convinced that any eligible woman will fall in love sometime during those years, and if she is not surrounded by the proper young men, who knows? She

might eventually marry a Yankee. And then what would happen to the line?"

Rule #3: Shoes and jewelry—that's it.

"Grandmother was convinced that clothes were a fraud. A woman could cover her body any way that she wanted, and it made no difference. She would be judged now and forever by her shoes and her jewelry. Therefore, pay attention to both."

I found the list short, sweet, and pointed. Still I felt I had to ask, "And what, as a contemporary grandmother who has seen so much of the world, would you add to your grandmother's basics?"

She thought carefully for some minutes. "Just one thing," she said at last. "Don't frown. It does terrible things to your face and disposition.

"And one more piece of advice. Definitely investigate wax injections."

MOLLY IS A GENIUS AND OTHER FAMILY TRUTHS

She was two months old when I visited her one day in her baby sling (or whatever her mother calls that piece of canvas slung across a wire frame). Perched on top of the kitchen counter, she seemed perfectly happy to be where the action was.

Her brother was lying on the floor making oatmeal cookies while his mother said, "Great, Max," and his father dropped flour in a bowl from above.

It was, as they say, just a typical Sunday.

But in the midst of this family bake-a-thon, Baby Molly was somewhat ignored, so I decided to talk to her. I leaned over the two-month-old lying there, her eyes darting about the room. "Hi, Molly," I said. Grandmothers seem to have a rather limited vocabulary. It is confined to words like "hi," "good," and "big."

"Hi," I said again. Now I had her attention. Her big eyes focused on me. "Hi," I repeated. "Hi, Molly. Hi. Hi."

Then she did it.

Molly looked straight at me and said, "Hi."

This is madness, I thought. A two-month-old baby does not say hi to her granny. "Hi," I said.

"Hi," said Molly. This time she gave me a big smile.

"Hi," I repeated.

"Hi," she said.

"Kathy," I said to Molly's mother, my voice quivering, "Molly just said 'hi.' "

"Oh, I know," Kathy said. "Isn't that wild? She does it all the time."

"She does it all the time, and you never even told me? You told me when she had a cold. You told me when she had conjunctivitis. But this? You never told me this. This is incredible."

"Well, it sort of is," Kathy admitted. "I took her to the pediatrician the other day, and he called the other doctors in to see her because she looked as if she were raising her head and trying to crawl."

"Crawl?"

"Yes, it's really kind of amazing."

"Why didn't you tell me?"

"It sounds too weird."

"Kathy, she probably is a genius."

"Do you really think so, Mom?"

I stopped.

Did I really think so?

Did I really think she would win the Westinghouse Science Award? Did I really think she would win The National Spelling Contest? Yes, of course. At that moment I knew she had it all.

I wanted to tell the world— or at least six other grandmothers I know who always want to tell me about their babies. But then I paused. What if she peaked at three months?

What if at the age of eight her longest word was still "hi"?

"Mom, what do you think?" Kathy asked again. "Is she a genius?"

I sighed. "It's too early to tell."

Kathy nodded. "That's what I think, too."

"At a year she may be behind all the other children."

"Right," she agreed.

"Now I know why you didn't tell anyone about 'hi,' " I said.

She smiled a wise and knowing smile.

"I think I'll just tell relatives," I said.

Kathy looked at me and shook her head.

"It's all right," I assured her. "They'll all think she takes after them."

A Star for Marisa

Marisa is a magic child.

No one knows quite why, but everyone agrees.

Still Marisa, at four, had to learn the difference between yes and no, the difference between sloppy and perfect, the difference between what she wanted and what Mommy decided.

So Marisa's mommy, with the wisdom born of being her mother's daughter, put a chart in Marisa's room.

The chart had a place for everything Mommy wanted Marisa to learn to do. There was a place for cleaning her room, a place for being polite, a place for shoe tying and buttoning and zipping. And next to each place was room for a daily star.

In order to turn the awarding of stars into a bit of a contest, Mommy suggested Marisa create a chart for her as well. Was Mommy as good as she should be? After all, if her parents expected perfection of Marisa, should she expect less of them?

"What shall we put on the chart?" Mommy asked.

Marisa considered a number of things and finally decided that Mommy would be able to get stars for such things as combing Marisa's hair without pulling it and hurting her, taking Marisa to special places, letting Marisa bake.

At the end of two weeks Marisa's mommy declared the experiment a great success. "It's wonderful," she said. "Marisa has a chart full of stars."

"And what about you?" Marisa's daddy asked.

"I haven't earned any, but I'm trying," she said.

What Marisa's mommy is really learning is that mothers and daughters are always harder on one another than the rest of the world is on either.

But it does take a lot of stars to see that.

THE BIRTHDAY GIRLS

t all began seven years ago with Marisa.

She was born in August, the first girl in our family born in August. And now we have a birthday quartet.

For Marisa's birth was followed two Augusts later by Stephanie's arrival. Two years later Elizabeth came to us, and then after another two-year wait came Molly.

So, with four granddaughters born in August, what's a grandmother to do?

You guessed it. Give a party.

I called Stephanie. "Dear," I said—I often call my granddaughters Dear or Darling or Baby because if I don't, chances are I will call them by their parents' names or the names of other cousins, brothers, uncles, and aunts—"Dear, would you like to have a birthday party at Grandma's?"

"Which grandma?" she asked. Stephanie does not fool around.

I explained that I would like to have a party for the granddaughters at our house in the country, and her next question was, "Will Marisa be there?"

Stephanie is not an easy sell.

The promise, however, of Marisa—and not just partying with

Marisa, but staying overnight and sleeping *with* Marisa—was the clincher.

"I'll go," she said.

Marisa and Elizabeth, who are sisters, were easier to convince. And Molly required no convincing at all; she goes where she's carried.

Molly and her brother Max came up a few days early with their parents. And the day before the party Stephanie arrived with her mother and brother; her father would come the night of the party. Marisa and Elizabeth arrived from Maine with their baby sister and mother. Within the next forty-eight hours two more fathers would arrive.

The day of the party the girls decorated the barn, had their pictures taken (they're on the jacket of this book), ran wild, took off their clothes, put on their clothes, jumped in the pool, threw balls, climbed stone walls, slid down rocks, picked flowers, sang songs, played games, blew out candles on four cakes, and some, along with their siblings, had their diapers changed. After all, we had seven grandchildren there, and five were still in diapers.

As the ice cream and cake were served, Kathy was in the barn with some of the children, and Denise was outside with others. Suddenly we heard Denise say, "OK, whose diaper needs changing?"

"Oh," Kathy moaned, her eyes rolling skyward, "please this once, just this once, don't let it be one of mine."

It wasn't.

But two minutes later it was.

Talking to my mother the next day I told her about the party, "And can you imagine," I emphasized, "we had eleven sleeping under one roof last night."

It was only after I put the phone down that I realized we had twelve.

But whoever said birthdays were for counting?

GRANDMA, THERE'S SOMETHING I HAVE TO TELL YOU

ost grandmothers are just recovering from the after-effects of motherhood, a pit stop on the road of life where kids in running shoes and tight jeans sit around on unmade beds looking like unmade beds.

It's a real shock to us to see that the slobs we raised are now parents themselves and are into such radical things as discipline and clean underwear.

And it's even more startling to find that these kids who responded to our questions about sex, drugs, and aberrant behavior with "I dunno. Who? Me? What?" when they were teenagers have raised a generation of nonstop talkers. As Pat, a today grandmother, tells it:

"I came home from a week in Europe, and just as we walked into the house, the telephone was ringing. It was Jeffrey, a freshman at college. Naturally I was very flattered that he would call his grandmother. Imagine! A world full of kids who do nothing but talk to one another, and he called me!

"Anyway, Jeff said, 'Gram, there's something I have to tell

you.' I didn't even have my bags unpacked, and there was Jeffrey ready to open his baggage. 'What is it?' I asked.

" 'Grandma, college is really different.'

" 'It certainly is,' I responded. 'You have a chance to meet new people, kinds of people you might not otherwise meet. And you're off on your own. How exciting for you,' I chirped with all the unnatural cheeriness of a TV newscaster.

" 'I don't think you get it, Gram,' he said.

" 'You mean you don't like college?' I asked. Now my heart sank. I could remember back in the Sixties when kids left school because they didn't agree with college policies. I can remember sit-ins and sit-downs and sit-ups, and I hoped he wasn't calling to tell me he didn't like the college's stand on Santa Claus.

" 'It's really strange, Grandma,' he went on. He didn't read my concerns over the telephone at all. 'I'm in a suite with three other freshmen,' he continued. 'One of them came in last night while I was studying and told me that he hates his father and wishes he'd die because he's rich and is sure to leave him a lot of money. And tonight another suitemate came in and told me he's gay, and I'm afraid what the third roommate will decide to confess tomorrow night. Listen, Grandma, I'm not so sure I like this school. Around here nobody's like us.'

"By the time we finished talking, I think I convinced Jeffrey that he had to be kind and helpful to the boy who hated his father and not condemn the boy who loved boys.

"Being like 'us' suddenly seems warm and comfortable to my grandson. And in that conversation I realized what 'us' does mean. Because we are a generation of grandparents that has been close to its grandchildren, because so many of us were so young when our grandchildren were born, we've had the chance to see them grow up. We've been a real part of their

lives, and I know now why they can call us from school and tell us the unthinkable, speak the unspeakable. We are even more experienced than their parents in communicating across the years. We learned a generation ago that if we wanted to get the confidence of kids, we'd have to soft-pedal our own ideas and subtly preach our ideologies. We got a lot of practice raising their parents and lowering our voices.

"When I put the receiver back on the hook, I felt very good about our family. I'm pleased that Jeffrey called me, and I was careful not to criticize but to listen and try to be helpful. I don't think I could have acted with the same coolness with my children.

"You know, I think I really was meant to be a grandmother. It was mothering that confused me all those years."

GIVE ME THIS DAY

monday, I think it was.

Every Monday my mother and her sisters took Grandma downtown for lunch, and then they sent her to the Palace Theater, where she could catch the first show (before the prices changed) and see the stage show and a new movie. A movie with, oh, maybe Carole Lombard or Irene Dunne or one of those other ladies my grandma and her daughters loved so much.

At lunch they probably exchanged recipes. The only thing I can ever remember my mother talking about with her sisters was what they made for dinner and how they made it. I suppose

they talked about all of us cousins, too, but I was never there so I don't know. I do know they couldn't have discussed anything of any importance to any of them because the unwritten rule in my mother's household was always, "Don't tell Mama."

Grandma had a heart condition (it wasn't what killed her in the end, of course), but everyone tiptoed through the major events of life because "just hearing that could kill Mama."

It was family legend that when my mother, the family baby, was pregnant with me, they didn't want Grandma to know the date Mother was due because "worrying could kill Mama." So the day I was born, my mother was in labor, and the two sisters took their mother to lunch and her show. When Grandma came out of the movie house, a friend stopped her on the street. "Congratulations," she said, "I hear your daughter just had a baby."

Even though Grandma proved that she could survive hearing about one of the great events in life from an almost stranger, the daughters still didn't open the channels of communication in the family. They continued to keep it all from Grandma.

I hadn't thought about "Don't tell Grandma" and the daughters' weekly luncheon date with their mama for years. It wasn't that I'd forgotten; I just didn't keep those memories at the ready.

Then my daughter Kathy had a daughter of her own. A few months later Kathy had a birthday, and as a gift I said, "Why don't I give you a day off with me? Why don't we go off and have a beauty day together? You know, massage and facial and all the fun things."

And so we did.

It was a treat to be together and talk about the condition of our nails instead of the condition of our lives. It was refreshing

not to be interrupted by squeaks and nursing and yelps for attention.

By the time the polish on our nails was dry and we were driving back to our individual everydayness, I said to Kathy, "I have a wonderful idea. Since we live in different cities, why don't we take a day a month to be together? Why don't you get a sitter for a day, and I'll take a day off, and we'll do something? It can be anything. We can go to a museum or a play or go out to lunch. But the rule is no children and no interference. Just us."

She agreed, and that's what we plan together.

It's not meant to be pretentious, just special in its warmth.

It took me some days before I realized that I am repeating history.

Like Grandma and her daughters, I am looking for that time when Kathy and I are together in the old mother-daughter sense and in the new companions-for-a-day sense.

Sometimes when I think about it I smile a little.

Despite myself, I am my mother's daughter.

And all this time I thought I was an original.

Sexy

Grandmas &

other Oxymorons

(Notes from all over)

SEXY GRANDMAS

Y ou do not have to be famous to be sexy.

Nowadays the shopping malls of America are stuffed with sexy grandmas.

Indeed, sexy grandmas are as common as head lettuce, and it is non-sexy grandmas who are the anomaly.

How can you tell if a granny is sexy?

She is a sexy grandmother if:

She goes out more than her daughter.

She complains less than her granddaughter.

She has friends of all ages.

She asks you why you're always tired.

Her nail enamel is brighter than yours.

She beats you at tennis.

She knows more about computers, astronauts, and football than you.

She talks more about her golf game than her gallstones.

She is refurnishing, redoing, or rebuilding something somewhere.

Her skirts are shorter than yours.

She is taking (or giving) a course.

When she doesn't sit for you, it's not because something hurts, it's because something's happening.

Her music didn't end when rock began, and she can recognize at least two current songs.

Grandma's Wardrobe

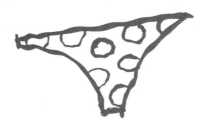

She isn't pouting because you didn't name the baby after one of her relatives.

She drives a car with a stick shift.

She can still wear two out of three: (1) a strapless dress; (2) a bathing suit; (3) high heels.

SEX AND THE
SINGLE GRANDMOTHER

f you are interested in staying gorgeous, consult a grandmother. She will probably tell you that the greatest invention since power steering is the pink light bulb.

The pink light bulb costs no more than the ordinary white light bulb lying there on your supermarket or hardware shelf, but once it goes into its socket, the pink bulb casts a magic glow. A little pink, and gone are the traces of youthful flings that are best forgotten. Gone are the reminders of middle-age mistakes that furrowed your brow. Gone are today's problems that turn down the corners of the mouth and make your face look like a smile poster turned upside down.

With a flick of a switch, a pink light bulb can erase more years than Estée Lauder with a six-month regimen.

Pink light bulbs, however, are just one of the props a grandmother needs to get along in a world that is obsessed with the big bosom, the flat stomach, and the tight tush.

In addition to pink light bulbs, a grandmother must have the ability to lie without laughing out loud. The lie, of course, is The Great Lie, the one about age. When someone asks how old you are, you answer with your daughter's age. Or you give your mother's age. Since people (no matter how good or bad you look) assume that you are lying, this is what is called The Safe Lie and can be used by grandmothers in business or when just foolin' around

It is also important for grandmothers to be conversant with the contemporary music scene. Nothing dates a grandmother faster than not knowing about any music since Frank Sinatra stopped recording with Nelson Riddle. The best place to learn the names of current groups is to turn on your radio (softly, please, and probably with earphones) to a station that calls itself easy rock, soft rock, hot rock, or just plain rock. Listen long enough to write down the names, commit them to memory, and whenever there is a lapse in a conversation between you and anyone young enough to know what you're talking about, drop the names of the newly learned groups. You will create a mild sensation.

The very best friend you can have, the friend who will make and keep you looking young, is your hairdresser. A good hairdresser will color your hair so that you look like the real you, only younger. A good hairdresser will cut your hair so that you look like the best possible you, not like a fashion magazine clone or The Haircut of the Week. In addition, a good hairdresser will look at all your pictures of the grandchildren and say clever things like, "This one has your eyes." Or "What a doll she is." Or "Cute boy." Doesn't matter that the hairdresser is cutting your hair and not even looking. What matters is that the hairdresser always says the right things, and then when the hairdresser is finished with you, he or she pats your head and says, "Who would ever believe you're a grandmother!" This statement alone is worth the large tip you will give your hairdresser.

As for cosmetic surgery, until they figure out a way to make a woman's hands look as young as her face—who's she kidding?

If young is your goal, gym is for you. But wait, don't rush there today. Do not go to any gym until you look good in a leotard. The leotard, incidentally, should always be black. So

should the tights. It must be understood that gyms are basically for women who do not look as if they need gyms. Gyms are for women who are already in such good shape that they go to the gym in order to show off their bodies. When your body looks as good as it's going to get, that means you're ready for gym. Now make sure you go to a co-ed gym before or after working hours.

When you are in need of getting in shape in order to look as if you are simply keeping in shape (we call this pre-gym), go to classes during the day. At 10 A.M. you can feel very good in a gym. You will definitely see bodies bigger and klutzier than yours, no matter how bad you think you look. This, of course, is a comfort. Besides, you know that you will graduate to early morning (we call this real gym) ahead of someone.

Early-morning gym is the time for executives and other rich people. Men and women on the fast track (literally and figuratively) are in gyms at 7 A.M. They run and row, and sometimes they stop for breath. It is when they stop for breath that you want to be there. The best place in the gym to meet a man is not swimming laps (who can talk when he's worried about breathing?) or running (same as with swimming). The very best place to meet a man is on the stationary bicycles. As one woman says, "It's great. They can't run away. You have a captive audience."

All of these things may not make you feel young and sexy, but they will cause other people to think you are as young as you think you look and as sexy as any other woman with moveable parts. As a result, you just may find yourself the man of your dreams.

Of course, there is one easy surefire way to make a grandmother feel young and sexy: Fall in love with a grandfather.

Is Your Grandmother Married?

hey had been together for a long time, so we teased her a lot about getting married.

"Hurry up," I used to say, "before the grandchildren start asking questions."

But, after a while when you see a small, hard smile instead of a ready grin, you know the time for teasing has stopped.

Still, even though they weren't married, they acted more married than plenty of people with nice gold bands and mortgages to match.

They gave dinner parties, went on trips, and complained about each other as much as any legally married couple. Furthermore, just like the rest of us wives, she went out in search of herself each Sunday while he sat in front of the television set watching whatever sporting event the networks decided to broadcast.

And then one spring day she blew the whistle on this man who couldn't say yes to marriage. For she was a woman who wanted to stop saying no to life.

"I'm going to leave you," she told him one rainy day. "It isn't that I don't care about you. I do love you, and I will always be your best friend. But I want to be in charge of my life, and as long as I stay with you, I know you'll decide what I do."

"Where are you going?" he asked.

So she told him. She was going to visit her sister, then come back to the city and finish some work she had begun earlier in the winter. Then she had a job in Europe, another in South America. She would be traveling a good deal, but in between she'd come back.

"Why are you telling me?" he asked.

"Because," she explained, "I think you'd better find someone else who will take as good care of you as I have these past years. I can't simply walk out without giving you some warning. I'll never talk about you with anyone, but if I did, you'd never have to worry. Because I do love you, but I must have a life that is mine."

He walked out the door and did not say another word to her.

She went to the telephone and called for her airline tickets, made her reservations, and began to pack her bags.

At five o'clock the doorbell rang, and he stood framed in the doorway, a box of flowers in his arms. "I want to marry you tomorrow," he said.

And so they were married.

"Why?" I asked. "Why, after all these years, did he want marriage?"

"Because for the first time I wasn't afraid of what he'd say or do, and I didn't play games with him. I didn't threaten to leave ever before. This time I simply told him quietly and without any histrionics that we were finished. I guess when a woman doesn't cry, it scares a man a lot more than when she rants and raves and sobs."

"Is it different being married?" I asked.

"Not for me," she said, "but the strangest thing has happened with him. He is different. His feelings about me are more tender, more open. He is more caring. He really is my husband."

"But you?" her friend persisted.

"I always knew how much I loved him. For me marriage is an extension of what I always felt. I think that for him marriage is an awakening."

Not surprising, is it?

Although we women are always assumed to be the romantics of the world, it is oftentimes men who are romantic and women who are pragmatic.

We women tend to marry the right men for solid, basic reasons: they are caring, paternal, good companions on the road of life.

Think about that for a minute, and then ask yourself:

How many women ever married a man because he had good legs?

An Unmarried Grandmother

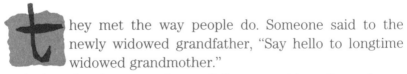hey met the way people do. Someone said to the newly widowed grandfather, "Say hello to longtime widowed grandmother."

And so they began a winter of dinners and benefits and parties.

From the start he was plainly enchanted.

She was a woman who radiated star power, something that

comes from within and is burnished to a high shine by the outside world.

And he was a man who radiated dollars—not all bad in a world of widows and orphans.

From the start she told him that she would never marry him. "But I'll give you thousands of dollars every month," he insisted. She just laughed and laughed. "That sounds like clamshells to me. I can't even translate that into how many dresses it would buy."

She wasn't teasing; she meant every word, but she noticed that his two grown daughters seemed a touch nervous. Not to worry, she assured them. "I promise I am not leading your father on. I have told him that I am not going to marry him, but I do like him very much, and I like both of you very much, and I hope we can all be good friends." Of course that was what happened.

What grown daughters can resist a widow who assures them she's not after their father and all his assets?

By spring the man was tired of fun and games.

"We will get married," he said to the widow.

"I'm afraid you didn't listen when I said no," she repeated.

"But I'm lonely," he said sadly. "I was happily married for so many years, and I like a woman in my house."

"I cannot be that woman."

"Then just come and spend a weekend in the guest cottage at my house," he insisted. "Just spend one weekend, and see if this isn't really the life you want."

"A weekend?" she asked, and as she spoke she thought to herself, "Why not? Why not indeed? Didn't my mother always say rich men made very good husbands?"

So off she went to the weekend retreat.

It was indeed a pretty little cottage on a vast and wondrous estate, and the widow settled herself comfortably.

At the end of the first day she realized she was lonely. At the end of the second day she knew she was very lonely, and at dinner the third day she told him that positively, definitely, absolutely she could not marry him.

For she had learned what she had always thought was true. She had learned that money really wasn't enough. And she had found out that the loneliness in life is not the result of being alone; it is the result of feeling alone.

The erstwhile suitor has pledged to find himself a wife, and he is looking now.

Our friend the widow wishes only the best for him. As for herself, she says, "Oh, I do hope his new wife will like me because I don't want to lose him as a friend—it's just that I don't want him as a husband."

And that is one of the great advantages of being a grandmother in the love game. You don't have to buy what you don't love.

Once you have your children and your sense of self, you can afford the independence that women with biological time clocks only talk about.

WHAT PRICE GRANDMA?

It was one of those hot July nights, and the room was heavy with the feeling that comes when you know the hostess's intentions are too big for her house.

I looked at my watch. It was too early to leave the party and

too late to see a grandchild. My husband was out of town, and I figured I had another hour to kill before going home to do something interesting like cleaning closets.

So there I was, standing on the terrace engaged in significant self-debate about staying or going when Gwen stopped to talk to me. We had met only a couple of times before, Gwen and I, but we sensed that we shared an I-wish-I-knew-you-better feeling.

"Alone?" she asked.

I nodded.

"Me too. My husband's away. Have you had enough of this party?"

She'd read my mind. "Want to go out and have dinner at a little place around the corner?" I asked impulsively.

"It takes me twenty minutes to say thank you," she said. "I'll meet you at the door in thirty minutes, and we'll go."

What I remember best about that dinner was that Gwen, who represented a kind of exotic bicoastal life I'd only read about, wanted to talk most about her children.

This woman who I thought was 92 percent glitz and glamour wasn't interested in telling me about her star-studded life. She was in town to visit her daughter who'd just had a baby. Gwen, who wrapped her body in the best designer clothes and went to parties of The Rich and Famous, was sitting across from me in a restaurant confiding the way it is with grown daughters— the more you love them, the less you say.

We talked about men and marriage and women and careers. But no matter how much we talked about our big world, the talk kept coming back to the little world of babies, the tiny world of grandchildren who did not yet walk or talk.

Gwen was not interested in passing along any of her famous

recipes or telling about her star-studded friends. She was en-amored of a baby, awash in the sentiments of generations.

"Let's get together again when I come here," she said at the end of the evening.

"Why not?" I said casually.

But inside I wasn't casual. I was rather pleased with me. A woman who led a champagne-and-caviar life shared a salad and diet soda with me, and we'd both had a good time. I learned a valuable lesson that night. I learned that all that glitters is not necessarily false. I learned that just because someone is rich and beautiful doesn't mean she isn't nice and doesn't know what's really important.

I learned that the very rich can also be very caring.

I suppose Gwen came to town after that dinner, but I never heard from her. In time I forgot about our dinner, and when I went to California, I didn't even think of calling her.

And then one day I picked up the newspaper, and there in black type was Gwen's name. She had died the day before.

I was shocked. How could she? Relatively young and at the center of such a colorful life, how could she leave it?

At lunch some days later a mutual friend told me about Gwen. "I remember when you and Gwen had dinner," she said. "You both told me about it. But what I knew, and you didn't, was that Gwen had been sick for five years. It was the best-kept secret on two coasts."

For weeks after I kept looking at the faces in the crowd. I still do. How many women—and men—with the good haircuts and $500 suits hide the secrets of life and death behind careful makeup and studied words?

How do so many of us endure what we are expected to accept without telling people?

And I have come to realize that my comfort level with Gwen was based on my not knowing her real life story. We were pleased with one another because we shared grandchildren, a special pride. It was enough for both of us.

Perhaps those grandchildren, those sweet legacies, are meant to be a unifying bond for us grandmothers —uniting us not only to the generations that are our family, but to the generation of our contemporaries so that finally, at our last chapter, the worldly accomplishments do not separate us. Instead the universal treasures unite us.

PERSONAL STORY

h elen always thought that when Harry left her, it would be in a pine box. Instead he departed in a late-model Porsche with a late-model product manager in his company.

For a year Helen's moods rode from happy high (when anyone told her that Harry was miserable with the new woman) to desperate low (when Harry called about speeding up the divorce so that he might be free to marry again).

It was the advice of her attorney to remain unemployed ("You get a good job, and it will affect your settlement") that left Helen so much time and so little activity.

Her married friends were busy choosing up sides, and it seemed to her that they were all on Harry's side. Well, why not? He had the social life, and she had—what did she have? She had a bitter lump where there used to be a heart. She had an empty place at the table, an empty place in her bed, and as she

looked around there was no way to fill the empty places.

Her married daughter and her son in law school were not much help. "Get out, Mom," they both said when they called. What did they expect her to do? Hang out in bars? Invite men to take her out? How did they think a woman who still considered herself married could go out and look for the next man? Why wasn't it easy for women the way it was for men? Why couldn't a woman just meet a younger man and take up with him the way men did with younger women? Didn't anyone understand that men between the ages of fifty and sixty were not out looking for women the same age?

And then one day Helen picked up a magazine, and there at the back in the Personals section was a series of ads she'd always glanced at but never read. Here were ads from single white males (conveniently shortened to "SWM") looking for women. Of course, for every ad from a man there were thirteen or fourteen from women. Still . . .

The one that caught her eye read, "California man wants to meet sophisticated New York woman 25–34 who knows books, theater, fine dining. Object: fun. Photo a must." There was a box number for replies.

In the era of AIDS and herpes, in the world of gay men and bisexuals, in the swamp out there that awaited newly single women, could Helen afford to risk answering?

On second thought, she counseled herself, what did she have to lose? You couldn't get AIDS in the mail, and besides, she wasn't 25–34. So, once he saw her, all would be lost anyway.

Helen went through her box of old pictures. Here was one from 1957 in a bathing suit. She could send that. Of course, in that picture she had long hair. Now her hair was short. Maybe she could get a fall. . . .

For three days she looked through old pictures, and just as she was ready to call a photographer, a letter came from her daughter. Inside were four sweet pictures of Helen with her two-year-old granddaughter Mavis.

Why not? she thought.

Helen went right to her desk and answered the man in California. She wrote:

Dear California Man,

If you want a truly sophisticated New York woman, please be advised that I know theater from the plays of Shakespeare to the musicals of Sondheim. I know restaurants from Soho to Harlem, and I know books from the Bible to this week's best-sellers.

So why am I writing to you?

Because, despite the fact that I'm loving, blond, and thin, despite the fact that I'm articulate and supportive, I couldn't hold on to my husband of thirty years.

There must be something wrong with me, and I want to know what it is.

You want a woman 25–34. My instincts tell me that only a man over fifty would want a woman 25–34. Well, I'm not 25–34. I am 25 plus 34. I am 59. Further, I am a grandmother.

Proof is this enclosed picture. The little girl is my granddaughter.

If all of this does not horrify you, please respond, and let's see if we can help one another.

I'll show you the New York you want to see, and you can show me where I went wrong after thirty years.

You see, I lost my husband to a woman 25–34 who

doesn't know what I know. But she does know one thing I don't know. She knows how to get my husband and keep him.

The answer came the following week.

A message was left on Helen's answering machine. "Helen," the voice said. "Until I read that letter, I didn't know what a dummy I'd really been. I'm the California man from the ad. I guess you know by now it's me, Harry. I'm ready to come back home. You see, you're wrong. That woman knew how to get me, but she couldn't keep me. I'm so tired of explaining who Keats is, and I'm tired of hearing that anyone who lived through World War Two must be in a retirement home. I think fifty-nine is a wonderful age to begin again. Besides, that picture really tore me apart. After all, I'm that little girl's grandfather."

GRANDMOTHER
WISDOM

ruth and Bernice went to Central High together, met their future husbands at the same party, and expected to live happily ever after.

In many ways they did, although both were faced with uncertain times. Married in the Roaring Twenties, they both survived the Depression of the Thirties and the war of the Forties. In the Fifties Ruth was widowed. In the Sixties Bernice was widowed, and by the time the Seventies rolled around, Bernice and Ruth

had returned to the same kind of dependent friendship that had first characterized their relationship.

Ruth and Bernice were both the mothers of daughters, but even though the daughters knew one another, the mothers had not created the kind of friendship that—like family silver—was handed from generation to generation, the patina growing richer with the years. Their four grandchildren knew one another not at all.

One day as Ruth was talking to her grandson, she mentioned Bernice's granddaughter. "I don't really know her," Ruth said, "but she might be a nice girl for you to take out some time." Ruth's grandson thought it would be "fun" (grandchildren either find things "disgusting" or "fun"). And so the grandchildren met, and in the time-honored tradition of movies and books fell madly, wildly in love . . . instantly.

The speed of it all made both grandmothers a bit tense, but neither would say that to the other. And if they had said anything to the grandchildren, which one would have listened? In less time than it took the grandmothers to buy dresses for the wedding, the marriage took place.

Ruth and Bernice swallowed their doubts and concentrated on their good fortune. After all these years, these two best friends who had felt like sisters all their lives were finally related.

But these jet-age grandchildren who fell in love so easily found that staying in love was more difficult than either expected. Their perfect marriage had been based on the theory of relativity—if their grandmothers loved one another, why wouldn't they? But friendship is not the same game as marriage.

It was ironic; the couple broke up before the wedding china chipped.

Ruth and Bernice sat down together.

What were they to do?

"I'll tell you," Ruth said, "that what my grandson does has nothing to do with my life. I didn't tell him to take your granddaughter out. I didn't tell him to fall in love with your granddaughter, and I didn't tell him to marry her."

"That's all true," Bernice agreed.

"You and I were friends before we had children, much less grandchildren. Are we going to let two grandchildren change a friendship?"

"No way," said Bernice.

"Good," said Ruth. "That's what I thought you'd say."

And what do Bernice and Ruth discuss now that their grandchildren are no longer married to one another? They discuss the great-grandchildren that were born to both of these grandchildren.

"You see," Ruth explained, "our grandchildren went on to marry other people, and both of them have satisfying marriages that have produced great-grandchildren. Just think if Bernice and I had taken sides when those kids were divorced. We wouldn't be speaking today, and meanwhile our grandchildren would have picked up their lives—as well they should—but our lives would have been shattered. You know, the longer you live, the more you learn that you cannot get emotionally involved in the lives of your children and grandchildren. You can hurt for them, but not with them. Divorce and losses—well, the children can recover from those blows. They have a lot more time and a lot more options than Bernice and I.

"It takes a really long time to learn that you can't let sex run your life forever. And now that we're both past all that silly sex stuff, wouldn't we be crazy to jump back in because of our

grandchildren and get involved once again in grand passions?

"It's very comfortable being us. And you know where we are? We're at the point in life where the most exciting thing is checking our answers on 'Jeopardy' every night and finding out we're still smart."

ON THE ROAD
WITH GRAMS

the two grandchildren call her Grams, but deep down she thinks of herself as Auntie Mame, a woman of the world who is willing to shlep her grandchildren anywhere in that world and give them a taste of the heady life she has known as both a high-powered career woman and the wife of a celebrated journalist.

Two summers ago, to introduce her granddaughter to the joys of Paris, the two packed up and went off to rough it. Roughing it with Grams means being put up at the best hotels, dining in the finest restaurants, and going to museums and places of interest. With Granddaughter it also meant a shopping spree. "After all," Grams asked in her singular rhetoric, "can anyone take a teenage girl to Paris and not teach her to shop?" So Granddaughter was given her own budget for shopping.

True to her word, Grams took Granddaughter to Printemps, the French store that thinks it is Bloomingdale's. "Oh, look," Granddaughter exclaimed, "may I buy this? And this? And this?" Grams assured her she could buy it all—if she were to pay for it. In the end Granddaughter decided to borrow money

from Grams and repay her at the hotel. But when they returned with their packages to the hotel, Grams—who may be Auntie Mame on the outside but is a stern disciplinarian on the inside —said to Granddaughter, "Before we go to lunch, you and I have a small accounting matter to settle."

Granddaughter's eyes filled. "You're not giving me these?"

Grams, melting but resolute, held her ground.

"Let me think about it overnight," Granddaughter said.

And sure enough, in the light of a new day, Granddaughter realized that she did not want to shoot her whole spending allowance at one store.

Grams, full of her role as teacher of values, determined to carry this lesson all the way. "I am not taking these things back for you," she said. "It's your job."

So, after breakfast, Granddaughter went off (she does speak perfect French) to return her purchases. Granddaughter was due back at noon to meet Grams at the hotel.

Noon came. No granddaughter.

Twelve-thirty. No word. No child.

Grams was hanging out the window, running up and down corridors. What if something were to happen to this child? What would she do? What would she say to Granddaughter's mother, who had trusted her?

One P.M. Where was she?

At 1:30 Granddaughter came in the door. "Oh, Grams," she said, "those French just won't let you return anything. I've been arguing for an hour. But I knew you wouldn't let me back if I didn't get it done. So I stayed."

Grams hugged and kissed her.

And from that day to this, Grams has never tried to teach her granddaughter a lesson in anything. "Let her mother do the

disciplining," Grams sighed. "I'm here for the fun."

And with that lesson for herself firmly in mind, the next summer Grams scooped up her grandson, the tennis aficionado, and trotted him off to Wimbledon.

"I know you dress casually," Grams said (amazed at her own ability to dismiss the sloppy look he affected with such ease), "but when we visit my English friends in the countryside, I do think that you will have to come to dinner wearing a jacket and tie. Nothing fancy, mind you. Gray flannels, a blazer, and any of your father's ties will do just fine."

And so the pair went off to the country, Grams with her long dresses and Grandson with his young American look.

The first night Grams sat down with Grandson. "Their grandson is coming to dinner to meet you," she said with an unusual touch of nervousness. "Now don't be nervous. He'll be very nice, I'm sure. And don't be upset if he comes in wearing a tuxedo. These people are very British and very proper, and I do think it's good for you to get a look at young people in other countries."

That evening Grandson not only was clean and presentable; he combed his hair, brushed his teeth, and practiced a polite, diffident smile which he thought Grams would find "very British."

He came down to dinner, sat in the library with Grams and her hosts, and awaited the grandson. But it was Grams who couldn't believe her eyes.

The English grandson entered wearing black-and-white-striped pantaloons, a huge checked shirt, and a floppy hat.

"Isn't he adorable?" asked his English granny.

Grandson winked at Grams.

Grams shrugged. "So I don't know everything."

HEEEEEEEERE'S
GRANDMA!

from the moment her daughter-in-law Linda called to say she was bringing Bobby, age two, to visit for a week, Janet beamed. She beamed even though the checkout person at the supermarket made a $2.20 mistake that she didn't catch until she got home.

She beamed even though the dripping kitchen faucet kept her awake for two nights.

She even beamed when she found out that no one had a crib to lend her, and she'd have to buy a collapsible one and store it in her non-storable apartment.

But look, this was her grandson. She had only one, and he lived with her son and daughter-in-law two thousand miles away.

This was her chance of a lifetime to play Grandma.

A whole week! Imagine what she could do with Bobby all to herself for a week. She'd tell him about this side of the family. She'd tell him about the grandpa who died before he was born. She'd take him to all the neighbors in her building. She might even take him to the restaurant when she went to work. No, this was one week she'd take off.

She smiled as she thought about it.

That's what she'd do.

She'd take a week of her vacation now, and if they wouldn't give her an extra vacation week after ten years of waitressing,

ten years of heavy trays and orders with a smile, then she'd show them and call in sick for a week.

In the end, however, they gave her the week (her boss had become a grandfather the week before), and her friend Dot came through with her brother-in-law's porta-crib.

It was going to be perfect. Janet would make it perfect despite the fact that her daughter-in-law Linda was one of those dust-free daughters-in-law who did everything better than her mother-in-law.

Linda cooked better, sewed better, decorated better, and undoubtedly was raising a child a lot better than Janet had. Janet sighed just thinking about her daughter-in-law. It was easy to admire Linda but hard to love her.

Not that any of that kind of competitiveness mattered today.

This week Janet was going to concentrate on winning over Bobby, not Linda.

Their plane arrived two hours late. Still Janet managed to smile when she saw them get off the plane.

Janet gave her daughter-in-law a peck on the cheek, held a squalling, sniffling Bobby (he did look like his daddy, didn't he?) up to be kissed, and he promptly wailed, "I wanna go home."

Linda shook her head. "He's not himself. He's had a cold for two days, and the airplane did terrible things to his sinuses."

Janet nodded sympathetically. "Just like his dad," she said consolingly.

"I think it comes from my side of the family," Linda said quickly. "We all have nasal problems."

Janet said nothing. Linda was so possessive about Bobby that he couldn't even inherit the rotten stuff from his daddy's side of the family.

The three—grim granny, rigid mommy, and cranky kid—waded through baggage claim ("But Linda, you don't have to carry it yourself. I'll get a skycap"), found the car (thank heavens the motor turned over), and began the drive. Then halfway home the heater conked out.

"I guess you can see what kind of trip this is going to be," Janet said half-jokingly.

"Unfortunately I can," Linda said. Then, quickly recovering her composure, she assured Janet, "It's not your fault—he's, well, he's just awfully tired and sick right now. And I'm sure you didn't plan to have the heater break."

Janet drove on in silence.

The first two days Bobby ran from Janet every time she tried to approach him. It wasn't that Linda was saying or doing anything to make him not want his grandmother; he really was a little boy with a stuffy nose who wanted his mommy.

The third day Linda said to her mother-in-law, "I thought I might visit my aunt, but I don't think I ought to take Bobby out at night—"

"I'd love to sit with him," Janet interrupted.

"Can you manage . . . could you handle . . .?"

"I'll try," Janet said. "I think I remember enough."

"I won't leave until he's asleep," Linda promised.

"I can put him to bed," Janet assured her.

"I think he'll expect me . . ."

Janet didn't say, "Of course he'll expect you; you won't let him expect anyone else."

Bobby had his milk, his nose drops, and his mommy—in that order—and went to sleep. Ten minutes later Linda went out the door.

Janet sat in her living room watching television, one ear tuned for a little boy's whimper from the next room.

Just before "Golden Girls," the sound came.

"Mommy. Mommy," followed by a plaintive cry.

Janet got up. She peeked in the door. "Grandma's here," she said.

Bobby looked at her and wailed loudly.

"Mommy's not here right now, but Grandma loves you, too," Janet assured him.

He shook his head and cried louder.

Suddenly Janet had an idea. "I'll bet you've never seen anything but 'Sesame Street' and 'Mickey Mouse,'" she said. "Well, kid, your grandma is about to broaden your horizon."

Before the next screech, Janet scooped her grandson from the borrowed bed, tucked him under her arm, and marched him into the living room.

"That's the couch," she said. "Your mommy calls it a sofa, but it's a couch. It's where I sit to watch television. And I look at junk TV, Bobby. That's all I turn to. I love soap operas and terrible miniseries and things that critics hate. I don't watch anything that's good for children or educational. And while I watch I eat popcorn. So relax, kid, you're with Grandma, and we're going to have a good time."

Just before the 11 P.M. news Bobby fell asleep, and Janet put him back in his room. When Linda came home, Janet assured her that Bobby was fine, just fine. She didn't mention their after-hours party.

The next morning Linda smiled so hard she almost cracked her plastic exterior. "Isn't it wonderful?" she asked. "He's so well-adjusted that he can sleep anywhere."

"In that case," said Janet, "why don't you make plans for tonight, too? I'm happy to sit with him."

"But it's so boring for you," Linda said.

"Oh," Janet answered truthfully, "I just like knowing he's nearby. It makes me feel good."

That night they watched the Movie of the Week and ate a milk-chocolate bar.

The next morning Bobby woke up and called for Grandma.

His mother went in to see him. "I want Grandma," he said, throwing his blanket out of the crib.

"Grandma's busy," his mother said, her lips pursed tightly.

"I want Grandma," Bobby said, banging his toy duck on the bed rail.

"Heeeeere's Grandma!" Janet said in her best imitation of Ed McMahon (they had watched a Johnny Carson rerun after the Movie of the Week).

Bobby screamed with delight and flung himself in Grandma's arms.

Four days later they left, and when they got to the airport Bobby cried and cried. "Me take Grandma," he sobbed. "Me take Grandma."

And then Linda, perfect unruffled Linda, did what she knew she had to do to get Bobby on the plane without creating a scene. She turned to her mother-in-law. "I think you'd better plan to visit us," she said.

Janet smiled.

She wouldn't go often. After all, they were two thousand miles away, and it did cost a lot of money, and she did have a job. Still there was something wonderful about a grandson who cried when he had to leave Grandma.

That's what it's all about, Janet thought as she picked up her pace through the airport. You could carry the trays and handle the complaints and work until your feet groaned out loud if somebody cried when you went away.

It wasn't so tough being a good grandma.

Just a week ago she hadn't known the secret.

But now she did.

Being a grandma just means having a good time.

The really amazing part was that winning the heart of a grandson wasn't really so different from winning the heart of any man.

What male ever failed to respond to a woman who was good to him?

What man ever said no to a woman who always says yes?

Then Janet laughed out loud.

Wait until Linda had to face her son at eleven o'clock tonight without the promise of a couch, hot chocolate, and Johnny Carson.

Grandmothers
are
to
LOVE

It's been more than twenty years since I published a little book called *Grandmothers Are to Love*.

I was decades from grandmotherhood, had just settled into motherhood, but still I thought that as a mother and reporter, I could see what grandmothering was about.

The little book was in print for more than ten years, and then it whirled without direction on the publishing merry-go-round until it was dropped.

When I decided to write this book about grandmothers, it seemed to me that *Grandmothers Are to Love* might make an appropriate coda.

And so, out of old loves and new understanding, but in slightly different form (because grandmothers now come in slightly different form) here is . . .

GRANDMOTHERS
ARE
TO LOVE

Here are some words
About somebody big
Who loves somebody little . . .

Oh, there are a lot of people
Who love you. . . .

The bakery lady
Who gives you a cookie,
Your uncle in Oscaloosa,
The next-door neighbor with bangs
Loves you
And so does
The dog across the street.

There are two second cousins
Who love you,
And your teacher
Thinks you are a dear.
The policeman, the mailman,
And the bus driver love you.

And ... oh yes ...
So do your mother and father.

But this somebody who loves you
Looks a little like a mother,
Smiles a lot like a father,
And has two pictures of you
In her purse.

This somebody who loves you
Makes good thick soup
And good thin cookies
And brings you sand from Florida.

This somebody who loves you
Takes you out to lunch
And invites you over to sleep.

This somebody who loves you
Shortens your clothes
And raised your parents.

This somebody who loves you
Dries your tears,
Tells you stories,
And shows you which one
Is the petunia.

This somebody who loves you
Holds your hand
When you hop the puddles,
Holds you tight
When you feel sad,
And holds you up
To see the parade.

This somebody who loves you is called
Mimi
Nana
Bubby
Noo-noo
Gamma
Gaga
Granny
or Grandma.

But no matter what you call her,
She's your grandmother.

And if you have a grandmother,
Aren't you the lucky one?
For grandmamas do many things
So grandbabies have fun.

When parents go away
Grandmamas do the sitting,
And if you need warm mittens,
Granny tends to the knitting.

If you have some clothes
That you call your Sunday best,
Chances are it's Nana's gift
That makes you so well-dressed.

But the gifts of clothes and seashells
That grandmothers think of
Mean nothing next to your gift,
The priceless gift of love.

For the most valued jewel of Grandma's
Is not a diamond or topaz,
But the precious little child
That her child now has.

You've a very special trust.
Remember this . . . please do,
The love of generations
Is handed down to you.

So if you have a grandma
Thank the Good Lord up above,
And give Grandmama hugs and kisses,
For grandmothers are to love.